Ben Franklin

Ben
Franklin

Printer, Author, Inventor, Politician

By Pamela Rushby

Founded in 1888, the National Geographic Society is one of the largest nonprofit scientific and educational organizations in the world. It reaches more than 285 million people worldwide each month through its official journal, NATIONAL GEOGRAPHIC, and its four other magazines; the National Geographic Channel; television documentaries; radio programs; films; books; videos and DVDs; maps; and interactive media. National Geographic has funded more than 8,000 scientific research projects and supports an education program combating geographic illiteracy.

For more information, please call
1-800-NGS-LINE (647-5463) or write to the following address:

National Geographic Society
1145 17th Street N.W.
Washington, D.C. 20036-4688
U.S.A.

Visit us online at www.nationalgeographic.com/books

For information about special discounts for bulk purchases, please contact
National Geographic Books Special Sales at ngspecsales@ngs.org

For rights or permissions inquiries, please contact National Geographic
Books Subisidiary Rights: ngbookrights@ngs.org

Library of Congress Cataloging-in-Publication Data

Rushby, Pamela.
Ben Franklin : printer, author, inventor, politician / by Pamela Rushby.
    p. cm. – (National Geographic history chapters)
  ISBN 978-1-4263-0191-9 (library)
1. Franklin, Benjamin, 1706-1790–Juvenile literature.   2. Statesmen–United States– Biography–Juvenile literature.   3. Scientists– United States–Biography–Juvenile literature.   4. Inventors–United States–Biography–Juvenile literature.   5. Printers–United States– Biography–Juvenile literature.   6. Authors, American–Biography–Juvenile literature.   I. Title.
E302.6.F8R88 2007
973.3092–dc22
[B]

                                    2007007896

Endsheets: A close-up of The Declaration of Independence.

Contents

In this portrait, Ben Franklin is shown as a scientist interested in the new field of electricity. The book he holds is titled *Electric Experiments*.

A Remarkable Man

As a boy, Ben Franklin liked to find new ways to do things. One day he noticed how his feet pushed him through the water as he swam. He wondered whether he could swim faster if he had bigger feet. So, Ben made wooden paddles and tied them to his feet and hands. The paddles did make him swim faster! Ben had made swim fins.

Ben's friends suggested that he might be an inventor when he grew up. Ben did become an inventor, but he was a printer, a writer, and a politician, too. He did important work for his government. Ben Franklin was a man of many talents.

Working in his father's candle shop, Ben poured boiling animal fat into molds to make candles.

Chapter 1

Early Life

Ben Franklin was born in 1706. He grew up in Boston, Massachusetts. He came from a large family. He had seven sisters and nine brothers. Ben was the tenth child and youngest son.

Three hundred years ago, some children didn't go to school at all. Ben was lucky because his father sent him to school for two years. Ben's report cards said he was good at reading and writing, but not at math.

Ben left school when he was ten, but he continued learning. He read books, magazines, and newspapers to learn more about the world.

He wanted to figure out how things worked. He studied writing, math, science, and languages. He learned how to steer ships across the sea by using the stars.

But Ben had to help out in his family's shop where they made candles and soap. The hot grease used for making candles had a nasty smell. The shop was always hot and smelly. Ben didn't like working there.

After work, young Ben Franklin would read by candlelight long after midnight.

Ben learned how to set metal letters and operate a printing press in his brother's print shop.

His father had an idea. Ben's older brother James had a print shop. This was a place where books and newspapers were printed. A print shop would be better work for a boy who loved books. When Ben was 12, he went to live with James and work in his shop. He planned to train until he was 21 to become a printer and then open his own shop.

Ben Franklin learned the printing trade as an apprentice in his brother's print shop. Later, he opened his own print shop, which became very successful.

Chapter 2

The Writer

James Franklin's print shop published a newspaper. Some of James's friends wrote articles for it. Their articles often made fun of important people. To keep out of trouble, they signed their articles with made-up names, like Ichabod Henroost and Fanny Mournful.

Ben wanted to write for the newspaper, too. He knew that James would never publish articles written by his little brother. So, Ben made up a new name: Silence Dogood. He even changed his handwriting. Late at night, Ben slipped the articles signed with his made-up name under the print shop door.

People in Philadelphia could buy newspapers, paper, ink, and other goods in Ben Franklin's shop.

Ben must have laughed to himself when James published his articles. When James found out who Silence Dogood really was, the brothers quarreled. They never got along after that. When Ben was 17, he ran away. He left Boston for New York, and then moved farther south to Philadephia.

Ben continued to write. He opened a printing shop and started his own newspaper by the time he was 24. Ben's paper *The Pennsylvania Gazette* went on to become one of the most successful newspapers in America.

Ben's Bright Ideas

Poor Richard's Almanack 1733–1758

One of Ben Franklin's most famous pieces of writing was *Poor Richard's Almanack.* During Ben's time, people didn't have many books. Many houses had only two books: a Bible and an almanac.

An almanac was like a calendar, but it also had recipes, jokes, songs, and clever sayings. *Poor Richard's Almanack* included sayings from a character Ben made up called Richard Saunders.

Some of his most famous sayings were:

"A penny saved is a penny earned."

"Three may keep a secret, if two of them are dead."

"Lost time is never found again."

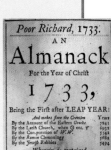

Chapter 3

The Scientist

As much as Ben loved writing, he was also interested in the world around him. He wanted to know how things worked and why things happened. The things he studied included diseases, the stars, hot-air balloons, ocean currents, and electricity.

Ben enjoyed experimenting. His most famous experiment took place in 1752. Ben proved that lightning is a type of electricity by flying a kite in a thunderstorm. Ben attached a metal rod to the top of the kite and a metal key to the bottom of the kite string.

◀ Ben Franklin filled his workshop with the latest electrical equipment and science books from Europe.

Franklin's kite experiment made him famous around the world. Harvard and Yale honored him for his scientific discoveries.

Ben believed that if lightning was electricity, its energy would pass through the metal rod. Then it would travel down the kite string to the key.

The storm's lightning didn't strike the kite directly, but Ben noticed that small threads on his kite string were standing straight out. Was electricity causing that? Ben reached out to grab the key. There was a hiss and a crackle. He jumped as a blue spark leaped from the key to his hand. It was electricity!

Experimenting with electricity is dangerous. Ben was lucky that day. He could have been killed if lightning had struck his kite.

Ben Franklin enjoyed trying out new ideas. He turned some of his ideas into great inventions. He had started out as an inventor when he made his swim fins. He continued to invent things all his life. Many of his inventions helped to make everyday life easier for people.

The Lightning Rod

Ben's experiments with electricity led to his invention of the lightning rod. This pointed rod was mounted on the roof of a building. Made of iron, the rod attracted the lightning and moved it through a wire safely into the ground.

Franklin placed a lightning rod, such as the one to the right, on top of this home. It saved the roof from catching fire when struck by lightning.

The Franklin Stove

In the 1740s, as Philadelphia grew, firewood became harder to find and expensive. The Franklin stove used less wood and heated a room better than a fireplace.

In Ben's time, a house was heated by a fire in an open fireplace. Most of the warm air escaped up the chimney instead of warming the room. So, Ben invented a stove for heating houses.

He made a big metal box and put it in the fireplace. He set fire to wood piled inside the box. Heat from the fire flowed out into the room. Cold air from the room flowed into the box and was heated. Soon, many American houses were heated by a Franklin stove.

Ben Franklin received no money for any of his inventions.

Bifocal Glasses

As Ben grew older, he needed to wear glasses. He had two pairs: one for reading up close and one for seeing things that were far away. Ben wondered if he could have two kinds of glasses in one frame.

Ben had the lenses of both pairs of his glasses cut in half. Then he stuck the lenses together. He put the close-up lenses on the bottom and the long-distance lenses on the top. The new glasses worked! When Ben looked down, he could see clearly to read through the close-up lenses. When he looked up, he could see faraway things clearly through the long-distance lenses. Now people only needed one pair of glasses instead of two!

The Catheter

Another of Ben's inventions still in use today is a catheter. Ben invented this device for one of his brothers who was very sick. A catheter is a thin tube that lets body fluids pass into or out of the body.

Modern-day catheters are made from a variety of materials, including plastic, rubber, and silicone.

Ben Franklin, first deputy postmaster general for the American colonies, hands mail to a post rider.

Chapter 4

Working for Others

We still remember Ben today for more than his inventions. When Ben was 42 years old, he decided to stop working at his print shop every day. He became interested in improving the way many everyday things were done. Some of these improvements are still in use today.

THE PHILADELPHIA CONTRIBUTIONSHIP
for the Insurance of Houses from Loss by Fire
— 🔥 —
Oldest fire insurance company in America. Founded in 1752 by Benjamin Franklin and his friends.

PENNSYLVANIA HISTORICAL AND MUSEUM COMMISSION

▶ Ben Franklin founded the first fire insurance company in America.

Reading became a popular pastime as the colonies set up public libraries like the one Franklin started in Philadelphia.

A Collection of Books

Books were expensive 300 years ago. There were no public libraries where people could borrow books.

Ben started a club called the Junto. The club members met to talk about the books they had read. Ben suggested that if the club members kept their books in one place, everyone could read all the books.

The club charged people a small amount of money to borrow the books. This money was used to buy more books. Ben's idea was the beginning of the first public library.

Hospitals and Schools

Poor people who couldn't afford to pay a doctor had nowhere to go when they were sick. Ben raised money to build the first public hospital in America. Ben also raised money to build a school for young people. He founded a college so that students in Philadelphia did not have to go to other cities to continue their education. In 1791, the college that Ben Franklin founded became the University of Pennsylvania.

Today, students at the University of Pennsylvania can sit down next to the man who founded their school.

A group in Philadelphia formed a firefighting company after reading a newspaper article by Franklin on ways to prevent fires.

The Fire Department

If a house caught fire in the 1700s, it usually burned down. There were no firefighters to come and put the fire out. Ben wanted to change this.

Ben set up the first fire brigade in Philadelphia. It was called the Union Fire Company. All the firefighters were volunteers who trained on their own time. Each man had his own leather bucket.

The men filled their buckets with water when there was a fire. They stood in a line and passed the buckets along to put out the fire. This was called a "bucket brigade."

The Postal Service

Ben had an idea how to improve Philadelphia's mail delivery. In Ben's day, mail wasn't delivered to houses. Letters were held at the post office until someone came to collect them. The problem was that people didn't know when a letter for them had arrived.

Ben suggested printing the names of people who had received letters in the newspaper. Then people would know they had mail waiting and could go get it.

In 1753, Ben became the deputy postmaster general for all the American colonies. He invented a machine  (shown here) called an odometer. It measured how far postal wagons traveled. It helped Ben find the best mail routes.

From left to right: Benjamin Franklin, John Adams, and Thomas Jefferson review a draft of the Declaration of Independence.

Chapter 5

Working for the United States

Ben Franklin was also interested in politics. He served in the Pennsylvania Assembly, which made the laws for the colony. At this time, Pennyslvania was one of 13 colonies ruled by the British.

In the 1760s, troubles began between Britain and its American colonies. By the 1770s, people living in the colonies became unhappy about being ruled by Britain. They wanted to rule themselves. Ben and other important colonial leaders joined to establish a new nation called the United States.

The French welcomed the famous American, Ben Franklin. They admired him as a scientist, an inventor, and a diplomat.

In 1776, Ben was among a group of people who wrote and signed the Declaration of Independence. It stated why the Colonies wanted to be free of British rule.

The American people fought the British in a war called the American Revolution. At first, the war didn't go well for America. Ben was sent to France to ask the French government for help. Ben got France to give the Americans the soldiers, guns, and money they needed to win the war.

The Americans won, and the United States of America was established as a separate nation from Britain. Ben Franklin helped draw up a treaty of peace with Britain. After nine years in Europe, Ben returned home to Philadelphia in 1785. He continued to serve his country. He helped write the Constitution of the United States. A constitution is a set of laws that states how a country is to be governed.

Conclusion

Ben Franklin died in 1790. He was 84 years old. He had been a printer, a writer, an inventor, and a politician. He worked for the benefit of others, and for his country. He was a remarkable man who was able to do different things well. Most of all, Ben Franklin was a man who had many bright ideas.

Ben Franklin and the other members of the Constitutional Convention approved and signed the U.S. Constitution on September 17, 1787.

Events in Ben Franklin's Life

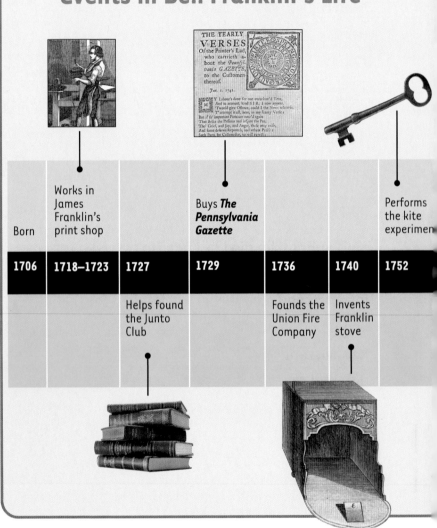

Born	Works in James Franklin's print shop		Buys *The Pennsylvania Gazette*			Performs the kite experimen
1706	**1718–1723**	**1727**	**1729**	**1736**	**1740**	**1752**
		Helps found the Junto Club		Founds the Union Fire Company	Invents Franklin stove	

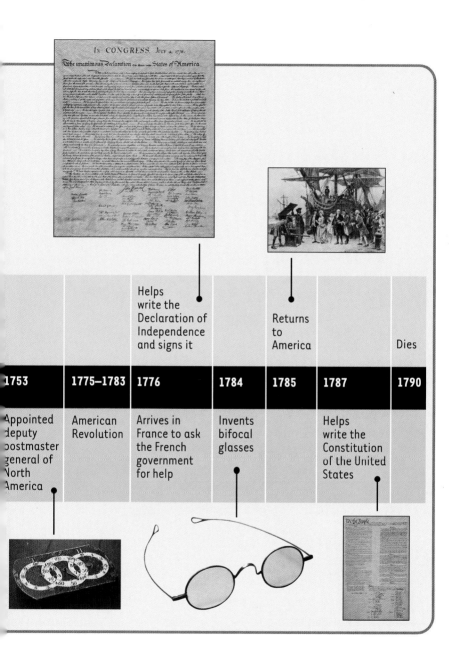

		Helps write the Declaration of Independence and signs it		Returns to America		Dies
1753	**1775–1783**	**1776**	**1784**	**1785**	**1787**	**1790**
Appointed deputy postmaster general of North America	American Revolution	Arrives in France to ask the French government for help	Invents bifocal glasses		Helps write the Constitution of the United States	

How to Write an A+ Report

1. Choose a topic.
- Find something that interests you.
- Make sure it is not too big or too small.

2. Find sources.
- Ask your librarian for help.
- Use many different sources: books, magazine articles, and Web sites.

3. Gather information.
- Take notes. Write down the big ideas and interesting details.
- Use your own words.

4. Organize information.
- Sort your notes into groups that make sense.

- Make an outline. Put your groups of notes in the order you want to write your report.

5. Write your report.

- Write an introduction that tells what the report is about.

- Use your outline and notes as you write to make sure you say everything you want to say in the order you want to say it.

- Write an ending that tells about your report.

- Write a title.

6. Revise and edit your report.

- Read your report to make sure it makes sense.

- Read it again to check spelling, punctuation, and grammar.

7. Hand in your report!

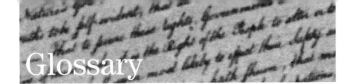

almanac	a book printed each year that includes useful information such as calendars and weather predictions
American Revolution	the war for independence fought by the 13 British colonies in North America against their British rulers (1775–1783)
article	a piece of writing in a newspaper or magazine
author	a person who writes a book, an article, or other kind of published work
catheter	a thin, flexible tube a doctor puts into a part of a patient's body
colony	a settlement that is far away from the country that rules it
constitution	a document that sets rules for how a country is to be governed
Declaration of Independence	the document that announced the separation of the American colonies from British rule
lens	a curved piece of glass in a pair of eyeglasses
odometer	an instrument for measuring distances a vehicle travels
politics	the business of governing of a country
treaty	a formal agreement between countries
volunteer	a person who does something to help others for little or no pay

Further Reading

• Books •

Barretta, Gene. *Now & Ben: The Modern Inventions of Benjamin Franklin.* New York: Henry Holt, 2006. Grades 2–5, 40 pages.

Editors of *TIME For Kids. Benjamin Franklin A Man of Many Talents.* New York: HarperCollins, 2005. Grades 2–4, 48 pages.

Fritz, Jean. *What's the Big Idea, Ben Franklin?* New York: Putnam, Reissue 1996. Grades 3–5, 48 pages.

Harness, Cheryl. *The Remarkable Benjamin Franklin.* Washington, D.C.: National Geographic Society, 2005. Grades 3–6, 48 pages.

Schanzer, Rosalyn. *How Ben Franklin Stole the Lightning.* New York: HarperCollins, 2002. Grades 2–4, 40 pages.

• Web Sites •

U.S Government Printing Office
http://bensguide.gpo.gov/

Franklin Institute Resources for Science Learning
http://fi.edu/franklin/index.html

Library of Congress
http://loc.gov/exhibits/treasures/franklin-home.html

ThinkQuest
http://library.thinkquest.org/22254

The Electric Franklin
www.ushistory.org/franklin/index.htm

Index

unanimous Declaration of the